IMAGES
of America

CHATTANOOGA'S
ST. ELMO

When Jesse Denny built her small shop in the corner of her yard at 4102 St. Elmo Avenue in 1919, she was not certain whether she wanted to open a gift or hat shop. Eventually, she settled on a hat shop. She held a contest to name her business, and "Ming Toy" was the winning entry. She eventually moved the Ming Toy into her home and moved the former shop to the back of the house. She operated the shop until the father of the current owner, James Lee, bought the home in the 1940s. (Courtesy of the Community Association of Historic St. Elmo.)

ON THE COVER: Members of the Thankful Memorial Episcopal Church gathered on December 9, 1923, for the consecration of the church by Bishop James Maxon. Although built 19 years earlier of pink limestone quarried on Lookout Mountain, the church's status as a mission of St. Paul's Episcopal continued for some time due to inconsistent enrollment and financial instability. It was built in part as a memorial to Thankful Johnson, and her youngest grandson, E. Foster Johnson, was confirmed on the day of the church's consecration. (Courtesy of the Community Association of Historic St. Elmo.)

IMAGES
of America

CHATTANOOGA'S
ST. ELMO

Gay Morgan Moore

ARCADIA
PUBLISHING

Published by Arcadia Publishing
Charleston, South Carolina

Library of Congress Control Number: 2012936547

For all general information, please contact Arcadia Publishing:
Telephone 843-853-2070
Fax 843-853-0044
E-mail sales@arcadiapublishing.com
For customer service and orders:
Toll-Free 1-888-313-2665

Visit us on the Internet at www.arcadiapublishing.com

*This book is dedicated to the citizens of St. Elmo, both
past and present, and especially to those who assisted and
supported the creation of this book. Thank you.*

CONTENTS

ACKNOWLEDGMENTS

A book such as this is never the work of one person. Many people are required to support and assist the one whose name will ultimately appear on the cover. It is, therefore, impossible to list here all of the individuals who have contributed to this history of the St. Elmo community. However, I would like to acknowledge some of the groups and individuals who provided special assistance.

First of all, thank you to the residents of St. Elmo, both past and present, who answered my many questions, related their family histories, entrusted me with their precious photographs, and invited me into their homes to share their St. Elmo memories. I deeply appreciate your patience and trust.

A number of individuals were of special assistance, including Jeff Webb, whose love of his community led him to collect and share many historical documents and photographs. It was Jeff's hope that this book would be written, and it could not have been without his assistance.

Special thanks go to the Community Association of Historic St. Elmo, whose excellent book and vintage photographs were invaluable.

Thank you to the staff of the local history department at the Chattanooga Public Library, who patiently shared their knowledge, expertise, and love of history. An added thank you goes to James Reese, who expertly scanned the many images from the library's photography collection. Thanks Jim.

Thank you to Barbara Chandler, superintendent of the Forest Hills Cemetery, who provided research and ongoing support.

I also wish to thank my Arcadia editors, Elizabeth Bray and Maggie Bullwinkle, for their professional guidance, support, and most of all, patience.

Lastly, thank you to my family, who encourage, tolerate, reassure, and occasionally prod. This is especially true of my husband, Sandy, who assumes the added tasks of proofreader and critic, not something I always accept graciously.

The photographs in this book are from the Chattanooga Public Library archives unless otherwise noted. Recent photographs were taken by the author.

INTRODUCTION

Prior to the arrival of white settlers, the area at the foot of Lookout Mountain was the intersection of two ancient Native American trails. The north-south trail traversed the east side of the mountain into Alabama. The east-west trail passed west of the Rossville Gap to the foot of the mountain above Moccasin Bend.

Early settlers also used the old trails. By 1805, the Georgia Road (St. Elmo Avenue) was built with the permission of the Cherokee using the north-south trail.

One early settler was Daniel Ross. A Scot, Ross was employed by trader and merchant John McDonald, eventually marrying McDonald's daughter, Mollie. The couple had nine children. Living in various locations in what is now St. Elmo, Ross built a wharf at Chattanooga Creek and traded with white settlers as well as the Cherokee. He was eventually made a member of the Cherokee Nation. Mollie and Daniel's youngest son, John, was the principle chief of the Cherokee during the forced removal of the tribe from Tennessee in 1838.

Following the removal of the Cherokee, the State of Tennessee assumed control of their land, establishing the Ocoee Land District. The property was sold in large tracts for as much as $7.50 to as little as 12¢ per acre.

In 1820, the federal government designated two post roads at the intersection of the Native American trails and established a post office. The area was initially referred to as Cross Roads and later Kirkland, after the major landowner in the area, Elisha Kirklin. A small community grew up around what is now the Incline.

James Whiteside purchased large tracts of land from the state following the removal of the Cherokee. Indeed, Whiteside owned much of the top of Lookout Mountain. He was wealthy and was not pleased when his daughter Thankful eloped in 1857 with tinsmith Abraham Malone Johnson. Initially estranged from his daughter, the birth of twins a year later led to reconciliation. At his death in 1861, Whiteside left her 400 acres on the eastern slope of Lookout Mountain.

Prior to the Civil War, the popular novelist Augusta Evans visited Lookout Mountain, already a tourist area. Maintaining that the scenery reminded her of that surrounding the St. Elmo Castle in Naples, Italy, she set her popular 1866 novel *St. Elmo* in the area, describing the blacksmith shop, the springs, and the bridge crossing Chattanooga Creek.

In 1878, Chattanooga experienced a yellow fever epidemic. The city was nearly deserted as citizens evacuated to what was considered safer ground in the mountains. The Whiteside Turnpike, the only road up Lookout Mountain, was rough and steep, and the tolls were high. The epidemic served as the impetus for the construction of another turnpike up the mountain. Known as Johnson's or St. Elmo Turnpike, the future Scenic Highway opened in 1879.

Intending to establish a large farm by extending his wife's property, A.M. Johnson purchased the adjoining land. By the early 1880s, his holdings extended to the Georgia line. Realizing that the land was too exhausted for farming, he began dividing the property into one-acre lots in 1885. Calling the area the Eastside, he sold lots primarily intended for summer homes. By 1888, the name of the post office was changed to St. Elmo, even though it was still located on land owned by the Kirklin family.

Over the next 20 years, St. Elmo grew rapidly. The streetcar line from Chattanooga was extended, and summer cottages began to give way to permanent homes for those who worked in the various industries on the south side of the city. More affluent families built larger, more opulent homes, hoping to escape the heat of the city on the "cool side of the mountain." As part-owner and president of the Chattanooga Water Company, Johnson was able to see that a water main was extended the length of St. Elmo Avenue. Thus St. Elmo became its first suburb and for many years "the place to live" in the Chattanooga area.

Incorporated in 1906 in order to issue bonds for a new school, St. Elmo grew to into a tightly knit community of diverse residents and small businesses. Incorporated into Chattanooga in 1929, St. Elmo remained a stable residential community until the urban flight of the 1960s. (Note that when St. Elmo was incorporated, the numbers of the cross streets were changed to be consistent with the numbered streets crossing Broad Street. Thus First Street became Forty-first Street and so on. The house numbers did not change.) Having weathered hard times in the 1970s and 1980s, St. Elmo is currently enjoying a renaissance as historic homes are renovated and residents join in rekindling the spirit of their neighborhood.

This book is divided into eight chapters. The first highlights the early history of the community and some of its residents, while the second chapter focuses on some of the residents of St. Elmo from the early 1900s until the present. The third chapter includes a number of the small businesses in the community, as well as the major industries that provided employment to many residents. The civic and political life of the community is the subject of the fourth chapter.

In St. Elmo, teachers knew their students as well as their parents, and nearly everyone attended church. Schools and churches are the subject of chapter five. The two inclines and the railroads are closely linked to the development and ongoing history of the community. The inclines, roads, and railroads are the subject of the sixth chapter. Chapter seven centers on the Forest Hills Cemetery. Opened in 1880, the cemetery occupies 100 acres east of the community. Chapter eight tells the story of the flood of 1917, which inundated Chattanooga and the surrounding communities, including St. Elmo.

This book cannot tell the complete St. Elmo story, but it is my hope that it will serve as an entertaining tribute to the citizens past and present who make up this lovely and vibrant community.

One

EARLY HISTORY

Born in Scotland in 1760, Daniel Ross came to what is now St. Elmo in 1785. A merchant and a trader, he married Mollie MacDonald and set up a store trading with both Indians and whites. Their eldest son, John, became the principal chief of the Cherokee and accompanied his people when they were forcibly removed to the Oklahoma Territory in 1838 on what would later become known as the Trail of Tears.

Pictured here with his wife, children, and grandchildren, Elijah Thurman was granted a number of tracts of land from the Ocoee Land District in 1838. Thurman's property later comprised most of the land south of St. Elmo and an area just south of the Georgia state line. Shortly before his death, he deeded an acre of ground for a cemetery close to the state line. Thurman was the first person buried there in 1873.

This point at the corner of St. Elmo Avenue and Thirty-seventh Street marks the 1820 crossroads of the first two post roads established in Hamilton County. This is also the location of Aaron Hunt's blacksmith shop, described in Augusta Evans's book, *St. Elmo*. Two Native American trails met at the foot of Lookout Mountain; one preceded along the east side of the mountain into Alabama the other crossed the foot of Lookout Mountain above Moccasin Bend. Early white settlers built the Georgia Road (St. Elmo Avenue) about 1805.

The area around Incline No. 1 was originally owned by George Kirklin. The scene of a small settlement, the first post office established in the area was named for Kirklin. The 40 acres owned by Kirklin adjoined A.M. Johnson's original holdings at their northern and western borders.

The two-story structure on the right was a tavern and inn during the 1870s. Located in what was then called Kirklin, it was advertised as a "pleasant resort." An antebellum settlement close to this location, Cross Roads had a reputation that was, as A.M. Johnson wrote, "anything but savory . . . saloons being prominent, was a rendezvous for gamblers, horse racing, and chicken fighting, shooting games, and scraps."

Born in Gainesville, Georgia, in 1830, Abraham Malone Johnson came to Chattanooga in 1851. A tinsmith and later railroad superintendent, the ambitious and handsome Johnson courted and married Thankful Whiteside, the daughter of a wealthy landowner and early industrialist, in 1857. When the Civil War broke out, he joined the Confederacy and rose to the rank of colonel. In 1886, on land inherited by his wife, he began developing the suburb he named St. Elmo.

Named for her maternal great-grandmother, who was born during a storm at sea as her parents emigrated from Ireland, Thankful Whiteside was the daughter of James Whiteside and his first wife, Mary. Engaged to another man, she eloped with Abraham Johnson in 1857. Estranged from her father until the birth of twins a year later, she eventually inherited a 400-acre farm. The couple, who from all accounts were devoted to one another, had seven children.

Francis Marion Walker lent $50 to A.M. Johnson to elope with Thankful Whiteside. Putting up his watch as collateral, Johnson claimed it was the only time he ever borrowed money. Walker, eventually rising to the rank of general in the Confederate army, was killed in the Battle of Peachtree Creek in July 1864.

A.M. Johnson built this 12-room redbrick Victorian-style home on Alabama Avenue at the foot of Lookout Mountain in 1887. Named Thankful Place after Johnson's wife, the home, which featured a tower and tower room, was considered one of the finest in the area. After Thankful died in 1890 and A.M. in 1903, their daughter Fanny Johnson Everett lived in the home until it was destroyed by fire in 1956. The site remains vacant today.

This panoramic 1903 photograph shows St. Elmo three years before its incorporation as a town. However, founder A.M. Johnson made certain that the community had a music hall located on

Augusta Evans Wilson set her most successful novel, *St. Elmo*, in the valley east of Lookout Mountain. She claimed that area reminded her of the countryside surrounding St. Elmo Castle in Italy, shown in this early-1900s postcard. The popular novel sold a million copies within four months of publication. The description of several area landmarks made it a natural choice when A.M. Johnson selected a name for his new town.

St. Elmo Avenue and community center located on Alabama Avenue. Later, a town hall was added on St. Elmo Avenue.

The most successful woman novelist of her time, Columbus, Georgia, native Augusta Evans Wilson wrote *St. Elmo* in 1866. In 1853, she stayed in the Lookout Mountain Hotel, owned by James Whiteside, where she met Thankful Whiteside. She returned to the area later to nurse her brother, who was wounded during the war. Considered an apologist for the South, her earlier books were reputedly banned from Union camps. *St. Elmo* was the basis of a play of the same name. It was staged in New York in 1910 and by the Peruchi Players at the Chattanooga Little Theatre in 1946.

This 1890 view of St. Elmo from the Valley Road (Tennessee Avenue) at Fourth (Forty-second) Street shows the Methodist church on the left and the Douglas Everett home on the right. The community grew rapidly as a result of the streetcar route as seen here and availability of water from the Chattanooga Water Company, partially owned by A.M. Johnson. Johnson added to his wife's initial inheritance with the purchase of large parcels of land from the Kirklin family and James Rawlings, among others.

A.M. Johnson is pictured here in front of his home with four of his grandchildren, from left to right, Thankful and Malone Everett (in back of cart), Bryson Webb (driving the cart), and Foster Johnson (standing). Also pictured are the dog Dock and the donkey Cyclone. (Courtesy of the Community Association of Historic St. Elmo.)

16

By the 1890s, the area from today's Fifty-second Street and Virginia Avenue to the Georgia line was called Mountain Junction. The community had over 200 residents and was the terminus for the trolley that ran through St. Elmo, the Belt Line, and the Broad Gauge up Lookout Mountain, as well as the line that went into Alton Park. This photograph shows the interurban railroad line, which ran from Chattanooga into the suburbs, including St. Elmo.

A.M. Johnson apparently enjoyed being with his children and grandchildren. He is pictured here, on the far left, with six of his grandchildren as well as other children riding on the firsr-prize-winning Children's Float in the Chattanooga Spring Festival in 1898.

Mary Jane and railroad contractor Adam Poe were given this home at 5410 Tennessee Avenue, pictured here about 1895, as a wedding present from her father, Congressman William Crutchfield. Crutchfield owned a farm over the Georgia state line that eventually became the Patten family farm, called Ashland.

John Rawlings came to Chattanooga in 1852. Apprenticed as a druggist, he enlisted in the Confederate army, serving in the medical department. After the war, he married Annie Moore and worked for a number of druggists, eventually going into business with his brothers. Their Broad Street store is pictured here in 1892. Rawlings was instrumental in founding the Chattanooga Humane Society in 1884. Rawlings and his family lived in St. Elmo.

A successful businessman, John Rawlings eventually helped found the Lookout Sewer Pipe Company. He owned a number of acres in the Kirklin area in what was to become St. Elmo. Located at the present site of the Incline parking lot, his home was the site of a lawn party in 1886 that A.M. Johnson asked Rawlings's wife to host to celebrate of the naming St. Elmo. The party, similar to one described by Augusta Evans in her book, was lit by large torches placed in boxes of sand. (Courtesy of the Community Association of Historic St. Elmo.)

Charlotte and George Washington Patten, older brother of Z.C. Patten, lived in this home on Old Wauhatchie Pike. He moved his family from Illinois in 1883 to assist his brother in operating the Chattanooga Medicine Company. He served as general superintendent of the company for 25 years. The family of his son, John A. Patten, also occupied the house. (Courtesy of the Community Association of Historic St. Elmo.)

A Union veteran who survived the Confederate prison at Andersonville, Georgia, Judson Mossman moved his family to Chattanooga from Maine after the war and built this home at 5307 Beulah Avenue in 1885. The home features a mansard-style roof, more common in the northeast. Mossman's youngest daughter, Clara, lived in the home until her death at age 102.

In addition to modest homes, a number of those made wealthy by Chattanooga's industrial boom of the 1880s and 1890s built homes in the area, including George Wheland and George Scholze. The grandest was Thankful Place, seen here from the rear. Built in 1887 by A.M. Johnson in the area he originally called Eastside, the home was located on property that was part of his wife's inheritance. It was one of the first in Chattanooga equipped with a furnace. The interior featured hand-carved cherry and golden oak woodwork and stained-glass windows.

James Whiteside Johnson, second son of A.M. and Thankful, married Sue Cleage in 1886. As a wedding present, the senior Johnson gave the couple a plot of land at the corner of Forty-third Street and Alabama Avenue on which to build this home. James was affiliated with several industries in Chattanooga and was active in political affairs. The couple had seven children. All of the children except the oldest were born in the home. (Courtesy of the Community Association of Historic St. Elmo.)

Finley Seagle, seen here with his wife, Mary Alice, came to Chattanooga in 1883. Initially employed by the Chattanooga Lumber Company, he purchased the company in 1892. Active in community affairs, he was a member of the chamber of commerce, Red Cross, Community Chest, Optimist Club, and the Chattanooga Automobile Manufacturers Association. He was an elder in the Cumberland Presbyterian Church for over 40 years. As mayor of St. Elmo during the 1917 flood, Seagle's actions were instrumental in rescuing many citizens of the community.

Finley Seagle (seated in the center), pictured here with members of his extended family, was one of the original St. Elmo town commissioners, serving as treasurer for 17 years and mayor for eight. Like all of the town officials, he served without pay; he believed that those who did so were more dedicated and efficient. He was particularly instrumental in building Lookout Mountain Junior High School and the South St. Elmo Elementary School. The Seagles lived on Tennessee Avenue at Forty-seventh Street, where they reared their eight children. (Courtesy of the Community Association of Historic St. Elmo.)

The community grew rapidly as a result of the streetcar route and availability of water from the Chattanooga Water Company, partially owned by A.M. Johnson. Additionally, the valley east of Lookout Mountain is cooler than downtown Chattanooga, thus offering a summer refuge for those escaping the heat of the city.

Two

RESIDENTS

This 1906 view of Thirty-eighth Street shows the St. Elmo Colored School to the west and the Patten Memorial African Methodist Episcopal Church behind it on the left. St. Elmo had a black community centered around Forty-sixth Street east of St. Elmo Avenue, an area known unofficially as Gamble Town. A number of residents owned grocery stores, barbershops, and other businesses, including blacksmithing. Robert Hankins owned the store at 4508 Tennessee Avenue. Others worked as domestics, gardeners, and laborers.

When this 1906 photograph was taken, Dr. Abraham and Mary Boyd lived here at 424 Wauhatchie Pike. Dr. Boyd, a physician and surgeon in practice with his father-in-law, W.B. Well, discovered a cure for pellagra. Prevalent in the post–Civil War south, pellagra is correlated with poor nutrition. Dr. Boyd founded a company that manufactured a cure for the condition. Mary Boyd was active in the Francis Marion Walker Chapter of the United Daughters of the Confederacy, the St. Elmo Book Club, and the parent-teacher association.

When Jane Bates died at age 90 in 1946, she was hailed as the "mother of Chattanooga." Not only was she a mother to her own four children, she also founded the first parent-teachers association in the Chattanooga area at the Louis Sanderson School. According to the Reverend Paul Martin, who delivered her eulogy at the St. Elmo Methodist Church, "she held a motherly interest for everything and everyone around her." She was a Sunday school teacher, a writer and historian, and "had a great understanding for people and their problems."

Horace and Alice Humphreys built their home at 4700 Tennessee Avenue in 1904. Initially employed with the railroad, Horace entered public office. He served as a justice of the peace, Hamilton County sheriff, election commissioner, and prohibition enforcement agent. Alice grew flowers in the couple's backyard greenhouse, eventually opening a florist shop at Eighth and Cherry Streets. Humphreys Florists continues to operate today under the ownership of their granddaughter, Helen Humphreys Johnson. (Courtesy of Helen Humphreys Johnson.)

This pre-1889 Victorian farmhouse at 4409 Alabama Avenue was built by the Arnold family, who operated a dairy farm. The Malcolm Bice family owned the house for over 40 years. Bice was a longtime employee of the Incline.

James and Susan Sizer reared their six children at 4517 Alabama Avenue. The couple is pictured here with four of their children, (from left to right) Nancy, Burnet, Octavia, and Hilda. One of the most distinguished lawyers of his day, James Sizer successfully defended the Coca Cola Company against charges that Coca Cola contained a "narcotic" (cocaine) and should be banned. His firm included Tennessee Supreme Court justice Alexander Chambliss and Sen. Estes Kefauver. (Courtesy of the Community Association of Historic St. Elmo.)

Burnet Sizer and his wife, Edna, built this home at 4515 Alabama Avenue next to that of his parents. The homes shared a rock wall garden. Having served as a marine in France during World War I, Sizer eventually joined his father's law practice. The couple had two sons, James and Seth. Although this home is still a residence, the James Sizer home was destroyed by fire. (Courtesy of James Burnet Sizer III.)

James and Grace Doyle reared their children, Patricia and Jimmy, at 4716 Florida Avenue. While serving in the Army during World War II, James receiving the Bronze Star and oak leaf cluster. Following his discharge from the Army, James worked at the Chattanooga Hardware Store, while Grace maintained their home. The children attended the South St. Elmo School. Patricia relates that during World War II, the grocery store across from the school somehow occasionally managed to acquire Hershey bars. Children would stand in line at the store to buy the precious 5¢ chocolate bars. (Courtesy of Pat Shadden.)

Pfc. William Holmes, a resident of St. Elmo, died on December 24, 1944, while rescuing his shipmates from a sinking troop carrier in the English Channel. He was awarded the Soldier's Medal for heroism and is buried in the Chattanooga National Cemetery. A sheet metal worker before the war, he left behind his wife, Nancy, and mother, Mrs. W.K. Holmes Sr.

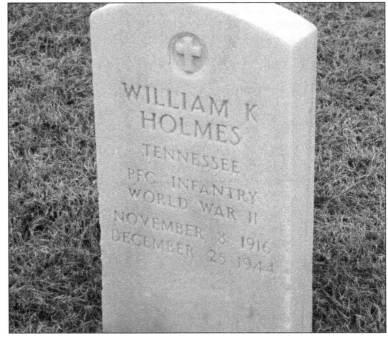

J. Santford and Elsie DeBerry moved to St. Elmo from Alabama in 1942. The couple and their five children purchased a home at 5601 Tennessee Avenue. Santford worked for the Crane Company, while Elsie was eventually employed at the Uniform Rental Company on Tennessee Avenue. The family attended the St. Elmo Baptist Church for a time, where the couple sang in the choir. (Courtesy of Gail DeBerry Satterthwaite.)

Penelope Johnson Allen was the oldest child of James and Sue Johnson and granddaughter of A.M. and Thankful Johnson. During her lifetime, she was a beauty queen, teacher, wife, mother, hotel manager, respected journalist and newspaper editor, historian and noted genealogist, munitions plant supervisor during World War I, and indomitable traveler well into her ninth decade. She remodeled the carriage house behind her parents' home on Alabama Avenue and lived there much of her adult life. She died at age 98 in 1984.

Jim and Lois Lee, shown here on their wedding day on March 24, 1943, met while Jim was in pharmacy school in Birmingham, Alabama, and Lois was obtaining a teaching degree. Following World War II, the couple returned to St. Elmo and joined Jim's father and uncles in what had been his grandfather's pharmacy on Broad Street. Living originally in the small house behind their current home at 4102 St. Elmo Avenue, the couple is among St. Elmo's most loved and respected citizens. Their home was once the Ming Toy Hat Shop. (Courtesy of Jim and Lois Lee.)

Jim "Doc" and Cordelia Lee owned the Lee Drug Store on Broad Street. Moving to St. Elmo in the 1920s, the family lived for a time on Tennessee Avenue, eventually buying a large frame home at 109 Ochs Highway. The couple had the house renovated and completely bricked. Doc and Cordelia are pictured here during World War II with Vic Vincente, an Army buddy of their son, Jim. Eventually becoming the Pettit House Bed-and-Breakfast, the home was demolished during the April 2011 tornadoes. (Courtesy of Jim and Lois Lee.)

Located at 4104 St. Elmo Avenue, this four-square home was assembled on site, probably in the 1920s, from a kit purchased from Sears and Roebuck. From 1908 until 1940, Sears shipped over 70,000 such homes via railroad to sites all over the United States. The homes, often with more than 30,000 pieces, included all the material necessary to build the house. Such homes included modern amenities like indoor plumbing, central heat, and electricity.

Peyton and Mamie Alley and their sons Ernest and Roy lived at 5407 Beulah Avenue. Peyton was a railroad maintenance superintendent. After her husband's death, Mamie taught for a number of years at Pineville Elementary School. (Courtesy of Robert Alley.)

Ernest "Herc" Alley played football for Baylor School and the University of Tennessee at Knoxville. He is pictured here in his uniform about 1929. After college, he coached high school football in Greenville, Mississippi, winning a state championship. After a brief time at Middle Tennessee State College, he was hired in 1940 by Vanderbilt University as an assistant coach. In 1943, acting as interim head football coach, he led the team to its only undefeated season to date. He continued to coach at Vanderbilt until 1971. (Courtesy of Robert Alley.)

Dr. Sidney and Myra Wood reared their three children—from left to right, Beverly, Sidney, and Peggy—at 4104 St. Elmo Avenue. Although he maintained an office in the James Building, Doctor Wood had an emergency office in his home. People who had been involved in fights and accidents often came to his home at night, where he treated them with no questions asked. (Courtesy of Sidney Wood.)

Naval aviator and Golden Glove heavyweight champion Sidney Wood is pictured here with his mother, Myra. Educated at the University of California–Los Angeles and Peabody University, Mrs. Wood established the first kindergarten in St. Elmo in her home. Her husband, Doctor Wood, often picked up the neighborhood children for school and returned them home in the afternoon. (Courtesy of Sidney Wood.)

Fidesah Ingram Alexander taught in the Chattanooga School System for 32 years. When she retired, the city honored her by naming the corner of Tennessee Avenue and Forty-third Street in her honor. Her first husband, Fain Ingram, taught at the Cave Springs, Georgia, School for the Deaf and later owned Fain Ingram Company, located at 1710 South Market Street. (Courtesy of Angie Peele.)

Ina Ruth Ingram Peele spent much of her life in the stone house at 4300 Tennessee Avenue purchased by her parents, Tidesah and Fahn Ingram, in the 1940s. She attended the University of Cincinnati on an opera scholarship and later taught piano. (Courtesy of Angie Peele.)

Reared in St. Elmo, Sharon Skipper Allen, pictured here at East Gate Mall with her Pinto race car, raced with the International Motorsports Association (IMSA) in the early 1970s. She set a women's world closed course speed record, 155 miles per hour, in an IMSA RS-class race. Her car is housed at the International Motorsports Hall of Fame in Talladega, Alabama. (Courtesy of Sharon Allen.)

Jeff Webb has lived most of his life in St. Elmo. His family, including his six sisters and two brothers, spent much of their childhood at 4310 St. Elmo Avenue. They attended South St. Elmo School and Lookout Junior High School. As a boy, Jeff delivered newspapers in the community, pulling his red wagon. He continues to live in his beloved community. He is a St. Elmo historian, while his wife, Alma, is a skilled genealogist. (Courtesy of Jeff Webb.)

National Football League Hall of Famer Reggie White spent much of his childhood in St. Elmo. A graduate of Howard High School, he was a defensive lineman for the University of Tennessee. His professional career included stints with the Philadelphia Eagles, the Green Bay Packers, and the Carolina Panthers. An ordained minister and devoted family man, he gave of his time and talents helping the children of the community. He died of a lung ailment in 2004 at age 43.

Three

BUSINESS AND INDUSTRY

This montage was created for the 125th anniversary celebration of the founding of the Chattem Corporation. In the center on horseback is Mrs. H. Lee Grimm, who traveled across several states collecting testimonials of women who used Wine of Cardui and Syrup of Black Draught. (Courtesy of Chattem Corporation.)

Founded in 1879 by Z.C. Patten, Fred Whiel, H. Clay Evans, and Theodore Montague, the Chattanooga Medicine Company (Chattem Corporation) moved to its present St. Elmo location in 1891, when the Patten family assumed full control of the company. The employees of Chatanooga Medicince Company are pictured here in 1913. (Courtesy of Chattem Corporation.)

The Chattanooga Medicine Company's first product was the laxative Black Draught. The company went on to produce a number of patent medicines, prescription medicines, chemicals, and food products. Pictured here are, from left to right, Latitia Franklin, Ethel Jones, Callie Forrester, and Ethel Harwood packaging Tincture Gentian for the US Army in December 1940. (Courtesy of Chattem Corporation.)

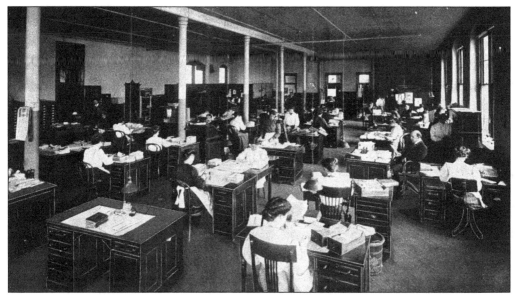

Wine of Cardui, a product marketed to women for menstrual pain, was a tonic with a sedative (alcohol) and an herbal antispasmodic. Company president John Patten died in 1916 while pursuing a libel suit against the American Medical Association's claim that the product was of no medicinal value. The company prevailed. The office of the Chattanooga Medicine Company is seen here in 1907. (Courtesy of Chattem Corporation.)

The Chattanooga Medicine Company published not only calendars and almanacs but also the *Ladies Home Magazine*. Fred Peay (left) and Newell Fry (right) are seen here in 1931 printing the magazine. The press printed 40,000 sheets a day. (Courtesy of Chattem Corporation.)

Until the early 1970s, Chattem Corporation ran its own printing shop advertising its products with calendars, Ladies Birthday Almanacs, and songbooks. The volume of advertising made the company the largest generator of mail in Chattanooga; as a result, the company had its own post office on the premises. (Courtesy of Chattem Corporation.)

During World War II, Patten Food Products, located on St. Elmo Avenue, turned out 34,000 packets of K rations for use by the US military. Chattem continues to do business at a number of sites in St. Elmo. (Courtesy of Chattem Corporation.)

Introduced in 1934, Charles Little's Seminole Flavoring Company took seven years to perfect the flavoring for Double Cola. One of the leading cola drinks in the United States and Mexico, Double Cola was the first bottler to use embossed letter bottles. The company moved to the location on Broad Street with its bright blue script sign in 1954. The building is currently occupied by Chattem Corporation.

German-born Robert (pictured here) and Gertrude Scholze came to St. Elmo in 1870. Initially, they operated a dairy farm, but soon Scholze started a tannery on Broad Street. The tannery prospered, and the couple built a large home on Old Wauhatchie Pike where they reared their five children. The Scholzes were known for their generosity to their employees and to the children of the community. Gertrude donated their summer home on Lookout Mountain as a summer home for the children of the Vine Street Orphanage.

In the first months after opening his tannery, Robert Scholze carried water from Chattanooga Creek to fill his vats. Just six years after coming to the area, Scholze's tannery was prospering, and he added a saddlery. Although the tannery was destroyed by fire in 1930, the family continued to operate the saddlery for a number of years. It continues in operation today at the same location under different ownership.

Like a number of other former Union soldiers, Pennsylvanian George Washington Wheland, pictured here with his family in front of his home, came to Chattanooga in the 1870s. Having worked in his uncle's foundry business, he began his own factory. Initially specializing in gristmills and cane mills, the Wheland Foundry soon expanded into making engines and sawmills. Wheland's home was located in north St. Elmo at 216 Belleview Street. (Courtesy of Margaret Wheland Cate.)

A devoted family man, George Wheland enjoyed picnics at his home on Wauhatchie Pike with his sons and their families. Pictured here, from left to right, are Ned Wheland, Sarah Wheland, George E. Scholze, Mary Wheland, Lena Wheland, Charlie Wheland, Beth Scholze, George W. Wheland, Buddy Scholze, George Wheland, Hilda Scholze, Dorothy Wheland, Minnie Wheland, and Willard Wheland. (Courtesy of Margaret Wheland Cate.)

Until his death in 1929, George Wheland was active in his company, often walking from his home on Old Wauhatchie Pike to his office. During World War II, the company made guns and shell casings. The firm was awarded the Army-Navy "E" for excellence in 1943 for its 100-percent engagement in war work. Wheland Foundry was acquired by Gordon Street Sr. in 1945. (Courtesy of Margaret Wheland Cate.)

Having grown up in St. Elmo, Roy McDonald founded the Home Stores in 1924. By 1929, he owned a number of Home Stores in Chattanooga, including two in St. Elmo. He began the *Chattanooga Free Press* in 1933 as a free weekly shopping news flyer for his stores. Having acquired the *Chattanooga News*, by 1939 he was engaged full-time in newspaper publishing. His father, Frank, founded Red Food Stores, now Bi-Lo.

German-born and -educated Dr. Henry Berlin came to Chattanooga in the late 1870s, when he and his wife ran out of money during a visit to America. Eventually, he established one of the largest medical practices in Chattanooga from his McCallie Avenue office. Reportedly witty and personable, he was on the first medical staff of Baroness Erlanger Hospital. He lived in the first home on Johnson Pike, now Ochs Highway.

Born in Walton County, Georgia, in 1866, W.M. Smith initially learned blacksmithing from his father. In 1888, he opened a successful blacksmithing business in St. Elmo. In 1893, he went to St. Louis to further study his trade. He returned to St. Elmo to open an even more successful blacksmithing business.

This 1916 photograph of St. Elmo Avenue shows Incline No. 2, the St. Elmo Drug Company owned by Ray Blevins, the St. Elmo Market, Louis Freudenberg's Eating House, the Incline Garage, and the St. Elmo Bakery.

A number of families operated stores on St. Elmo Avenue. Among them in the 1930s was the John and Gertrude Stone family. The couple and their six children lived behind the store. (Courtesy of Clare Mulkey.)

Seen here in 1950s, Hollister's (formerly Harkers') Tourist Court was located at 4106 St. Elmo Avenue. One of several such tourist homes located in St. Elmo during the mid-20th century, Hollister's is currently a private residence.

The Glass House Restaurant, located on Broad Street at the present site of WDEF-TV, was part of a chain of restaurants opened along major highways in the 1920s. As cars became more dependable and roads improved, tourist travel became more popular, including trips to Chattanooga and Lookout Mountain. The Glass House Restaurant chain failed during the Great Depression.

This picture postcard shows the Mount Vernon Restaurant about 1954, shortly after it was opened by Guy Tombras. The Mount Vernon, looking then much as it does today, is known for its excellent food, including its signature amaretto cream pie and elegant dining rooms. It continues under the ownership of Tombras descendants Jeff and Cindy Messinger.

Opened in 1957 on St. Elmo Avenue, the Confederama housed a 480-square-foot electronic map of the Civil War battles fought around Chattanooga. The exhibit included 5,000 soldiers, flashing lights, and a smoking cannon, along with a detailed description of the battles. The museum was sold in the 1990s; it was refurbished and reopened as the Battles for Chattanooga Museum on Lookout Mountain.

Joe and Winnie Light owned the Big Rock Tourist Courts on Cummings Highway. This 1930s postcard indicates that the tourist court featured 26 separate units with inside lavatories, Simmons Inner Spring mattresses, electric heat, and hot and cold water. The couple lived on Wauhatchie Pike. Their only child, William, is one of the soldiers memorialized on the St. Elmo World War I monument.

The Rock Castle Tourist Court, located at the foot of Lookout Mountain and owned by H.C. "Pete" Hines, was described in 1938 by "Dorothy" in writing to the C.M. Woodward family in Columbus, Ohio, as "the grandest cabin . . . better than some hotel rooms—fine bed with inner spring mattresses—nicely furnished, private bath, gas and electricity, attached garage."

During the late 1940s and 1950s, Walter Lyzon traveled from his home in the Hamptons on Long Island, New York, to spend the winter in St. Elmo. A hat maker, he sold his custom-made creations from his home on St. Elmo Avenue. Lois Lee was part of his extensive clientele and still has a number of his lovely hats.

The Zahnd Dry Goods Store opened at Tennessee and St. Elmo Avenues in 1892. Bess Zahnd worked in the store along aside her husband, Chris, for many years assisting customers in choosing new apparel. An avid fly fisherwoman, she died in 2006 at age 99. The couple is buried in Forest Hills Cemetery.

The Wann Funeral Home was built in 1938 by the Works Progress Administration (WPA) as a community center for St. Elmo. It also housed the Craig Lodor American Legion Post No. 148 until the post's building was completed immediately to the north of the funeral home. Paul Wann established his funeral home at this location in 1964. It is currently owned by John Hargiss.

St. Elmo resident (5201 St. Elmo Avenue) and oil company owner William Patterson obtained a license to operate a radio station in 1936. He adopted the call letters WAPO, which stood for W.A. Patterson Oil. Originating from the second floor of the Read House Hotel, the station offered music and local programs like *Man on the Street* and *Lost and Found*. The station also offered free air time to local churches.

George Williams celebrated his 85th birthday in 1959 at his St. Elmo home with fellow members of the Chattanooga Half Century Club. The club was open to men who had worked in the city for over 50 years. Williams, who died in 1960, is seated second from the left. He was employed with Combustion Engineering and the Crane Company and was a fellow in the St. Elmo Masonic Lodge No. 673.

Manuel "Manny" Rico came to Chattanooga from Dallas, Texas, in 1970. Working for some years for Comolli Memorials, he and his wife, Barbara, opened their own monument company out of their home in 1985, eventually moving to the current location at the corner of St. Elmo and Tennessee Avenues. A 20-plus-year resident of St. Elmo, Manuel currently represents St. Elmo on the Chattanooga City Council. (Courtesy of Manuel and Barbara Rico.)

Located at Forty-ninth and Beulah Streets, the Martin Food Market was owned by Terry and Evelyn Martin (far right). Known for their high-quality meat, homemade chicken salad, and pimento cheese, the Martins often gave out free candy and had an above-ground swimming pool and whirligig next to the store. Irene Hassler (left), Evelyn's sister, worked in the store, as did their granddaughter Susan (center), who served as greeter when she was just a few weeks old and went on to be a cashier. Susan learned to drive delivering groceries. Evelyn was 103 in 2011. (Courtesy of Susan Martin Gilman.)

Ken Covey opened the St. Elmo Garage and Auto Repair Shop in the early 1940s on the site of a former blacksmith's shop. His grandson Donnie Covey operates the business today. Donnie is pictured here with "co-owner" Miles. For a number of years, a Texaco station operated across the street from the St. Elmo Garage. The location is now occupied by the Purple Daisy Picnic Café.

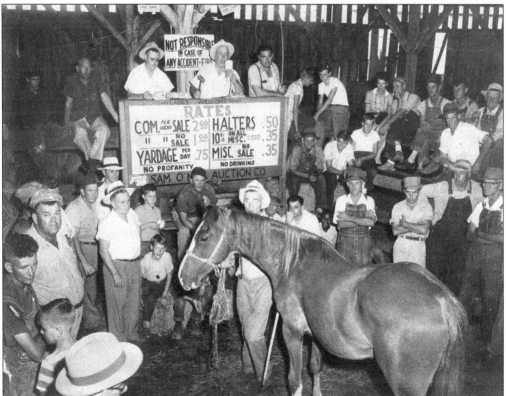

Sam O'Neil owned a horse and mule auction in the mid-1950s. Located at 3114–3116 St. Elmo Avenue from 1955 until 1973, he ran a number of businesses, including a horse and mule barn and a stockyard.

Pharmacist Martin McDonough Sr. purchased this home, located on seven acres on Tennessee Avenue, from the James Henderson family in 1944. The owner of the Incline Drug Company, McDonough opened his business in 1939 with $490 and a lot of determination. Following a hitch in the Navy, Martin's son, Martin Jr. "Buddy," joined him. Steve McDonough joined his father Buddy in the business and continues to be a pharmacist in St. Elmo. Incline Drug Company was located on St. Elmo Avenue at the current site of Blacksmith's Bistro.

In the early 1920s, Mollie White opened White's Grocery at 4900 St. Elmo Avenue. Soon joined by her sons, Henry and Tom, the name changed to White Brothers Grocery. The store was quite successful. The business frequently won contests sponsored by Sunshine Crackers and Grant Patten Milk. Grocery orders were often telephoned to the store and then delivered by truck or bicycle.

Four

CIVIC LIFE

St. Elmo's early town commissioners included, clockwise from top left, Finley Seagle, L.W. Bates, Reese Thomas (St. Elmo's first mayor), P.S. Poindexter, and Dr. H.B. Wilson. Incorporated in 1905, city ordinances prohibited gambling, keeping a house of prostitution, associating with a known prostitute, animal cruelty, doing business on Sunday, public intoxication, carrying or discharging a firearm, erecting a sign advertising a patent medicine or other article which might be offensive to ladies, and kite flying.

A small monument to St. Elmo commissioner and mayor Finley Alexander Seagle is located at the corner of Forty-eighth Street and Virginia Avenue. Bill Knowles is shown here at the monument with his son, William Finley Knowles Jr. (Courtesy of Bill Knowles.)

Born in Wales, Arthur Reese Thomas immigrated with his parents at age four. Settling at Blowing Springs, Georgia, he later served the Confederacy as a member of Watts Cadets and later Gen. John B. Floyd's cavalry division. After the war, he and his brother opened a department store on Market Street. He lived at 4202 St. Elmo Avenue and served on the first board of commissioners in St. Elmo.

When Minnie Wheland was elected to the Hamilton County School Board in 1916, a newspaper article described the first woman elected to public office in the county as "young charming, bright and happy, but still taking life seriously." Well-educated and always beautifully dressed, she held office in a number of local and national civic organizations. In the late 1920s, while on a trip, she was elected mayor of St. Elmo. Surprised, she declined the office but agreed to serve as secretary. (Courtesy of Margaret Wheland Cate.)

Squire L.W. Bates and his family moved to 3727 St. Elmo Avenue in the early 1890s. Active in civic affairs throughout his life, he served as St. Elmo postmaster, justice of the peace, school director, school board member, and mayor. He is credited with helping to improve South Broad Street between Chattanooga and St. Elmo.

Although the actual post office remained on Kirklin property, the name of the post office was changed to St. Elmo in 1886. The first letter carriers were not government employees; instead, they were former slaves Tom and Celie Jones. The elderly couple lived in the servants' quarters of the Johnson home, shown here. Having collected the mail for their route at the post office, since neither could read or write, each household looked at the mail, taking what was intended for that address.

The first government-appointed postman in St. Elmo was Richard Brown. Named Postman of the Year, his prize included a trip to Washington, DC. His wife, Nancy, told him "not to take one step toward Washington" unless he bought her a new house. This photograph shows them in front of their home at 1504 West Forty-eighth Street. (Courtesy of the Community Association of Historic St. Elmo.)

Richard Brown delivered mail in a wagon pulled by his horse, Mollie, which he named for his sister-in-law. In the late 1890s, St. Elmo had mostly summer residents. Brown guided Mollie with one hand and delivered the mail with the other. (Courtesy of Claudia O'Leary.)

Starting in May 1898, Chattanoogans, including many St. Elmo residents, held an annual Spring Festival. A midway was erected on Market Street. Band concerts, art exhibits, bicycle races, and manufacturers' displays highlighted the three-day festival. The various fire companies vied to see which one could most efficiently put out large bonfires. The festivals continued for several years. This photograph shows the midway in 1910.

The highlight of the Spring Festival was the grand flower parade. In 1898, with Adm. George Dewey as an honored guest, an estimated 75,000 people lined Market Street to view the carriages and floats elaborately decorated with floral displays. Girls vied for the title of Spring Festival Queen. Suburbs, including St. Elmo, sent their own queens riding on imaginatively decorated horse-drawn floats. St. Elmo's queen in 1898 was Jane Henderson, granddaughter of Congressman William Crutchfield.

The history of the Archibald Faidley family dates back to the earliest white settlement in the Chattanooga area. The owner of the Arcade Publishing Company, he lived for a time in St. Elmo and served on the town commission.

Prior to the construction of the fire station at 4501 St. Elmo Avenue, the residents of the community had to depend on the Fire Company No. 2, located on Broad Street. Built in 1936, the St. Elmo Fire Station is a handsome Tudor Revival, multicolored, multi-patterned brick structure with half-timbering on the second floor. It served for over 40 years as a fire hall and fire department office and was sold to the community in 2009 for use as a community center.

Richard Rollins was fireman at St. Elmo Station No. 14 for 16 years. He told his family that while fighting a fire during a particularly cold winter, the hoses froze upright and his toboggan froze to his head. He is buried in the Police and Fireman Memorial section of Forest Hills Cemetery. (Courtesy of Sue Rollins Jones.)

Willis "Sonny" Jones (center), son in-law of Richard Rollins, was a fireman for three years and a policeman for 10 years. He also drove the Incline for two years and completed his career driving a bus for Southern Coach. Both men were St. Elmo residents. (Courtesy of Sue Rollins Jones.)

Four generations of the Case family served in the Chattanooga Fire Department. Capt. Jack Case, serving from 1928 until 1948, was the captain of Station No. 14 (St. Elmo) for much of that time. Lt. James Case served from 1950 until 1978, while Robert Case served from 1980 until 2007. Jake Case joined the fire department in 2008 and continues to serve. (Courtesy Betty Case.)

Moving to St. Elmo in 1912, Chattanooga mounted police officer Clarence Livingston, on the far right, was killed while attempting to prevent a robbery at an East Main Street saloon. The 35-year-old officer left a wife and three children behind. The citizens of Chattanooga raised money to buy a home for the family. Though she could have moved anywhere in the city, Monnie Livingston elected to stay in St. Elmo, purchasing a home at 4705 St. Elmo Avenue.

The St. Elmo Boys Brigade is pictured here in 1902 in front of the Douglas Everett home at the corner of Forty-second Street and St. Elmo Avenue. Included in this picture are Mr. Meil, Walter Gibbs, James Long, Ralph Wilson, Will Krichbaum, David Wilson, Robert Mixon, Miles Davis, Charlie Whihoite, Walter Hasty, Raymond Johnson, Ben Spearman, Dwight Taylor, Bert Hybeck, Mitchel Spoup, Clifford Betts, Harold Wilson, L'Roy Sanderson, Ed Shauf, and Capt. Arthur Lawson. (Courtesy of the Community Association of Historic St. Elmo.)

Located in front of Wann Funeral Home, a granite monument with a bronze plaque honors those men from St. Elmo who served during World War I. Of the 119 men from St. Elmo who served, five were killed in the line of duty: James Lodor, William Light, Arthur Mason, William Cummings, and Alfred Orr. Two oak trees were planted close to the monument to honor those who served.

This early picture of a group of young St. Elmo women includes, from left to right, Thelma Luper Smotherman, Hazel Elliot Cornwell, Sadie Elliot, Thelma Krischbaum, Ruth McCrory, Pearl Parham, and Margaret Frayer. Thelma Smotherman was married to a St. Elmo pharmacist and was, according to Jim and Lois Lee, an accomplished china painter.

This photograph shows the Wheland Foundry employees' baseball team in 1912. The team was part of the Manufactures League, formed the same year.

The St. Elmo Tigers had their locker room in the basement of the home of Dr. Sidney and Myra Wood. The team, organized by the boys themselves during World War II, played seventh-grade and eighth-grade school teams. The boys also spent their time roaming over the neighborhood and Lookout Mountain, collecting scrap metal, and playing war. (Courtesy of Sidney Wood.)

Adolph Ochs was only 20 years old but had already been in the newspaper business for five years when he bought the *Chattanooga Times* in 1878. By 1896, he was president of the *New York Times*. He promoted the establishment of Chickamauga and Chattanooga National Military Park and was the founder of the Lookout Mountain and Chattanooga Park. Ochs Highway was dedicated in his honor in 1931, following his $150,000 donation to improve the highway.

Two monuments stand at the base of Ochs Highway where it intersects St. Elmo Avenue. The larger commemorates the opening of Ochs Highway in 1931. The smaller monument commemorates the acquisition and opening of the 3,000-acre Chattanooga Lookout Mountain Park in 1925.

Peter Rudolph "Rudy" Olgiati and his family lived at 5400 Tennessee Avenue. Returning from service with Army engineers during World War II, he was appointed Chattanooga Public Works commissioner. He served as mayor of Chattanooga from 1951 until 1963, during which time the interstate highway system was constructed in and around the city. He was a deacon of the St. Elmo Baptist Church, a Mason, and a member of the American Legion. He is shown here with his wife and grandsons, as well as his son and daughter and their spouses. (Courtesy of the St. Elmo Baptist Church.)

The first Brownie troop in St. Elmo was founded by Leontine Skipper at the St. Elmo United Methodist Church. (Courtesy of Jeff Webb.)

William "Bill" Finley Knowles was born at home on Forty-eighth and Virginia Avenues on July 13, 1934. A newspaper article stated that he was the third son born to the Knowleses on the 13th day of the month. Claude Knowles, a traffic policeman, was previously employed by St. Elmo commissioner Finley Seagle. The couple chose their baby's name in honor of his former employer. Bill Knowles is Hamilton County's longest serving elected official. Elected in 1974 as county clerk, he is currently serving his 10th term. (Courtesy of Bill Knowles.)

The Roy Nelms family lived at 4708 Alabama Avenue. In 1988, Nelms was honored by the Tennessee Historical Commission for his work to help preserve and renovate St. Elmo as well as promote historical tours of the community. The park at the corner of Alabama and St. Elmo Avenues is named in his honor. As head of the St. Elmo Improvement League, he was instrumental in planting 36,000 daffodil bulbs along St. Elmo Avenue.

Five

SCHOOLS AND CHURCHES

Nannie Gothard, pictured with her 1952 South St. Elmo Elementary class, taught first grade at the school from 1920 to 1958. The daughter of Forest Hills Cemetery gatekeeper Henry Gothard, she was also the Sunday school superintendent at St. Elmo Methodist Church and president of the Francis Marion Walker Chapter of the United Daughters of the Confederacy. (Courtesy of Helen Humphreys Johnson.)

Tannery owner Robert Scholze became concerned about the education of the children in the south Chattanooga area and built a one-room school at his own expense. The City of Chattanooga reimbursed him and, in the 1870s, built the 17th District School, with Prof. B.H. Logan and his wife, Martha, as the principal and lead teacher. Professor Logan was the principal of the school for 22 years. Seen here during the 1917 flood, the school, located on St. Elmo Avenue and Thirty-eighth Street, was used as an emergency shelter during the flood.

About 1885, the 17th District School became a full high school. Sometime later, it was returned to use as an elementary school and renamed North St. Elmo School. It was later named the Louie Sanderson School in honor of its longtime principal, Mrs. Louie Sanderson, pictured here. Continuing as an elementary school for a number of years, the school was torn down in 1974. The site is now occupied by the Sun Trust Bank. (Drawing by Sahara Raines.)

By 1891, it was obvious that St. Elmo needed a new school in the southern part of the community. A.M. Johnson donated a lot at the corner of Forty-seventh Street and Alabama Avenue. A musical production at the district hall, located at the corner of Forty-fifth Street and St. Elmo Avenue, was organized to raise funds to build the new school. The first building was a frame structure that was moved across the street to become the community music hall when the brick school was built in 1906.

St. Elmo was incorporated in 1905 in order to sell bonds to build a new school. Built in 1906 using the best materials available, the three-story brick South St. Elmo School was designed by C.D. Adams. The first-grade class of 1911–1912 is pictured here with its teacher, Katie Price, and Principal Stacey Nelson. (Courtesy of the Community Association of Historic St. Elmo.)

The St. Elmo Colored School opened in 1903. Located on West Thirty-eighth Street across from the Chattanooga Medicine Company, the school was a two-story building with a bell tower. One of its early principals, William Hale, became the founding principal of the Tennessee Agricultural and Industrial State Normal School in Nashville in 1912. In 1927, Hale was elected president of the National Association of Teachers in Colored Schools. (Courtesy of the Community Association of Historic St. Elmo.)

Thirkeld Cravens, a graduate of Clark University, began his teaching career at the St. Elmo Colored School in 1927. He also taught at Calvin Donaldson Elementary School and Howard High School. Although the records are incomplete, it is quite likely that African American students living in St. Elmo began attending Calvin Donaldson School when it was opened in early 1926.

By 1915, the community had outgrown the smaller redbrick school, and a cream-colored brick addition was built. School pictures taken on the steps of this addition show the two-story columns with the American flag flying between them. A 1957 addition housed a cafeteria and auditorium. Pictured here is Elizabeth Moore's second-grade class in 1953. The school is currently an apartment building owned by Alexian Brothers. (Courtesy of Jeff Webb.)

Herbert Kaiser was principal of the South St. Elmo School from 1952 until 1984. Among his many achievements at the school was the creation of the hopscotch and other games painted on the floor of the school. These games were used for recess on rainy days. The school's indoor playground was featured in *Life* magazine in 1960. (Courtesy of Jeff Webb.)

In 1922, Mayor Findley Seagle proposed building a new high school that would serve both St. Elmo and Alton Park to the Hamilton County government. The county judge, Sam Connor, proposed a junior high school instead, a rarity at that time, if the communities could raise money for the land. Seagle purchased the property by persuading the community of Lookout Mountain to join in the project. Lookout Junior High School opened in 1925.

Located on 22 acres, Lookout Junior High School offered a full curriculum, including foreign languages, mathematics, English, civics, hygiene, science, history, industrial arts, music, art, physical education, home economics, and athletics. Creed Bates was the first principal of the school. The school closed in 1974 and is currently used by the Hamilton County School System for administrative offices.

Creed F. Bates, son of Lafayette and Jane Bates, was the first principal of Lookout Junior High School and the principal of Chattanooga High School for 37 years. He served in the US Army in World Wars I and II, rising to the rank of colonel. A beloved and respected educator, he was dedicated to helping his students achieve. Standing in the back row, second from the left, is an 18-year-old Bates with the 1912 Lookouts baseball team.

Following his completion of a program in timepiece creation and repair at the Bowman Technical School of Horology in Pennsylvania, Jim Pettit opened a clock repair shop and the Chattanooga Horological Institute in his home at 113 Ochs Highway. Over the next few years, he operated his institute and clock repair business from various locations in St. Elmo. He and his wife are currently living in Dublin, Ireland. (Courtesy of Jim Pettit.)

A.M. Johnson donated the lot on St. Elmo Avenue and Forty-second Street and funds to build the St. Elmo Methodist Episcopal Church. The first organized congregation in St. Elmo, this simple white frame church was completed in 1887. Sixty-one members were received into the congregation during the first year. Because there were no other churches in the community, the Episcopalians and Presbyterians worshipped with the Methodists. (Courtesy of the Community Association of Historic St. Elmo.)

As the St. Elmo Methodist Episcopal congregation grew, a parsonage was built in 1893 to accommodate a full-time minister, as opposed to a circuit minister.

Like St. Elmo itself, the congregation of the St. Elmo Methodist Church exerted leadership outside of its borders through its well-educated and influential members. The Methodist district parsonage was located at 5110 Alabama Avenue about 1909.

Known as St. Elmo Methodist Church, South until reunification of the denomination in 1936, by 1921, having welcomed home all 38 of the soldiers it sent off to World War I, the church had outgrown the old building. In 1921, it began construction at a site at Forty-seventh Street and St. Elmo Avenue. On March 5, 1922, the congregation paraded singing from its old church to the new church. The church was nearly destroyed in a fire in August 2009 but was restored and reopened in 2012. (Courtesy of the Community Association of Historic St. Elmo.)

The St. Elmo United Methodist Church parsonage was built in 1927 of the same dark red brick and limestone as the church located next door. Within a few years of completion, a pipe organ was installed in the new Methodist church. The growing congregation also organized a symphony orchestra composed of young musicians from the community and a drama club. (Courtesy of Jeff Webb.)

The history of the Baptist church in St. Elmo began in 1866, when a small group began meeting in a log schoolhouse. After meeting at various locations and under different names, the congregation built this white frame church at St. Elmo Avenue and Forty-fifth Street in 1906. The church continued to grow, and in 1928, the congregation purchased a large parcel of land across the street from this church. The St. Elmo Fire Station currently occupies this corner. (Courtesy of the St. Elmo Baptist Church.)

Members of the St. Elmo Baptist Church gathered at Burnt Mill on Chattanooga Creek to baptize new converts on August 3, 1902. (Courtesy of the St. Elmo Baptist Church.)

By 1928, the growing Baptist congregation purchased the land on St. Elmo Avenue to build this church. A new sanctuary, an education building, and additional meeting spaces were added as the congregation continued to grow. Still an active congregation, the church continues to minister to the St. Elmo community. (Courtesy of the St. Elmo Baptist Church.)

Rev. McKnight Fite was pastor of the St. Elmo Baptist Church from 1955 to 1968. During his time as pastor, all activities at the church increased, Sunday school enrollment rose to over 800, and the new sanctuary building was constructed. He is pictured here with, from left to right, his son Allan, daughters Sarah and Rebecca, and wife Nell in 1955. (Courtesy of the St. Elmo Baptist Church.)

Wenzola Kiger served the St. Elmo Baptist Church as Sunday school superintendent and historian, creating scrapbooks of church activities for over 20 years. Employed at Chattanooga Publishing Company, she was instrumental in establishing a credit union at the *Chattanooga Times*, serving later as the treasurer and secretary of the organization. She was also a writer, painter, wife, and mother. She is shown here in the 1950s receiving a gift of appreciation from the church presented by Dottie Lee and Barbara Garrett (at piano). (Courtesy of the St. Elmo Baptist Church.)

Organized with 33 members in 1889 as a mission church of the First Presbyterian Church of Chattanooga, the St. Elmo Presbyterian Church continues to play a vital role in the community. The church features decorative elements borrowed from the Queen Anne and Eastlake styles, with a gabled roof and elaborate exterior and interior wood treatments. It is considered one of the finest buildings in St. Elmo community. (Courtesy of the St. Elmo Presbyterian Church.)

The stained-glass windows of the St. Elmo Presbyterian Church honor, among others, Rev. Lachlan Vass and Mrs. Louie Sanderson. A former missionary to China, Vass was the pastor of the church from 1926 to 1942. Sanderson was the principal of the North St. Elmo School, which was eventually named in her honor. (Courtesy of the St. Elmo Presbyterian Church)

In 1944, W. Frazee, leader of a Seventh-Day Adventist medical group, came to St. Elmo to offer spiritual comfort and care for the sick. The group began holding meetings at the Incline Chapel on St. Elmo Avenue. By 1945, the group had purchased a house at 4015 St. Elmo Avenue, where it met until the 1970s, when it purchased the old St. Elmo Methodist Church.

A group of St. Elmo Christians was meeting in private homes when a tent meeting at the corner of Forty-seventh Street and St. Elmo Avenue led to the formation of the St. Elmo Church of Christ in 1913. The present building on St. Elmo Avenue, though remodeled over the years, was completed in 1914. The congregation continued to hold tent meetings until the 1950s as a means of attracting new members to the church. (Courtesy of John Smithson.)

The St. Elmo Missionary Baptist Church, located at 3701 West Avenue, celebrated its 150th anniversary in 2011. Originally located in a storefront, by 1905, the African American congregation had erected a church building across the street from its present location. Built in 1977, the current location boasts a paid-off mortgage and a congregation of 350.

Located at 3817 Church Street, the Patten Memorial African American Methodist Episcopal Zion Church was built in 1886 on land donated by C.Z. Patten. In the 1950s, the church boasted a membership of 200. Calvin Donaldson was among the founders of the church. When the congregation celebrated its 109th anniversary in 1995, there were only 20 members. The building was abandoned for some time but is now being restored.

Rev. William Fleming attended the Howe Institute in Memphis and Roger Williams University in Nashville before arriving in the Chattanooga area, where he pastored a number of churches including St. Elmo Baptist Church. He was also the longtime pastor of St. James Baptist Church on Duncan Avenue.

Established as a Sunday school mission of St. Paul's Episcopal Church in 1893, the property for Thankful Memorial Episcopal Church was bequeathed by A.M. Johnson at his death in 1903 as a memorial to his beloved wife, Thankful, who died in 1890. The first service in the pink limestone Gothic Revival church was held in 1906. The cornerstone was salvaged by Amanda Everett from the old St. Paul's Episcopal Church in downtown Chattanooga.

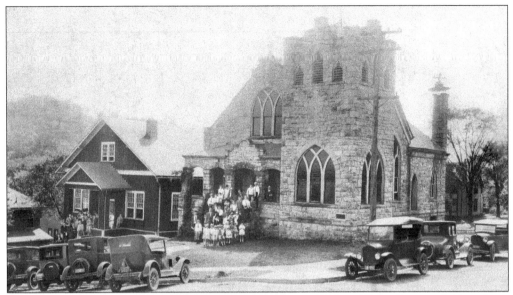

St. Mary the Virgin Episcopal Church began meeting in 1915 at Christ Episcopal Church on McCallie Avenue. The all-black congregation met there, according to diocesan records, "at a time not to conflict with white worshippers" until moving to a church on East Street and, later, to 4012 West Avenue. In 1995, the St. Mary's congregation merged with Thankful Memorial Episcopal Church, and the 1923 parish hall on the left was renamed in honor of the St. Mary's congregation. (Courtesy of Thankful Memorial Episcopal Church.)

The nave and sanctuary of the Thankful Memorial Episcopal Church remains much the same as when it was completed in 1906. The organ was donated by Christ Church of Nashville. The chimes were a gift to the church, but the church bell was "loaned in perpetuity" from St. Paul's Episcopal. A number of the stained-glass windows came from the home of A.M. and Thankful Johnson. (Courtesy of Thankful Memorial Episcopal Church.)

Pictured here in 1923, the members of Thankful Memorial Episcopal Church gathered for the consecration of the church by the bishop of Tennessee, James Maxon (second from the left on the porch). Rev. James Helms, BD, (second from the left in the last row) was the vicar of Thankful Memorial from 1923 until 1930. Also pictured is Mary Thankful Everett (at left in the fourth row). Miss Everett was the organist and music director of the church for 25 years. (Courtesy of Thankful Memorial Episcopal Church.)

By 1930, Thankful Memorial had 171 communicants, many of them direct descendants of A.M. and Thankful Johnson. During the Great Depression of the 1930s, Thankful Memorial saw a decline in numbers, but by the close of World War II, when the church saw over 40 members of the congregation in military service or the Young People's Service League, the church's membership had increased. This photograph was taken in 1923, when the church was consecrated. (Courtesy of Thankful Memorial Episcopal Church.)

Six

THE INCLINES, RAILROADS, AND ROADS

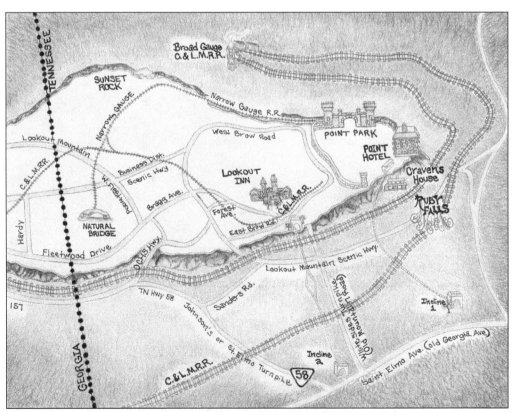

Although not drawn to scale, this map illustrates the relative locations of the roads, inclines, and railroads that operated in and around St. Elmo. (Illustration by Brandi Henderson.)

The first road up Lookout Mountain was a turnpike built in 1852 by James A. Whiteside. Seeing the potential for tourism on the mountain, Whiteside charged $2 for each wagon or horse using the turnpike. He also built the Lookout Mountain Hotel. Whiteside owned the point of Lookout Mountain, to which he charged a 25¢ admission. Later, his wife, Harriet, granted exclusive access to the turnpike to one livery service. The turnpike, now the Old Mountain Road, is visible in this 1955 photograph.

The fees charged to use Whiteside's Turnpike enraged both local residents and visitors, many of whom were Civil War veterans who wished to show their families where they served. Locals were further enraged when the fees remained in force during the 1898 yellow fever epidemic as many residents fled from the valley to the relative safety of the mountain. The turnpike is visible to the right of the Incline No. 1 tracks in this 1890s photograph.

In 1879, A.M. Johnson built a second turnpike that was cheaper and followed an easier grade. Called St. Elmo or Johnson's Turnpike, it was built to the south of his father-in-law's road and Incline No. 2. Ochs Highway follows the general path of Johnson's Turnpike.

In response to the Whiteside monopoly of the turnpike and lodging on the top of Lookout Mountain, in 1885 a group of citizens, including Maj. W.P. King, a US Army engineer, developed a plan to construct a cable car line from St. Elmo to the north side of Lookout Mountain directly below the point where the Whiteside Turnpike ended. They also planned to build a hotel tall enough to reach the mountaintop elevation in order to match the view from the Whiteside property. This photograph shows the Point Hotel and the valley below about 1888.

Pennsylvanian George Duncan was a Union veteran. George and his two brothers, James, an iron worker, and Sam, who worked for the Chattanooga Electric Railway, came to Chattanooga shortly after the Civil War. George was the general contractor for Incline No. 1. Duncan Avenue is named for Sam. (Courtesy of Roy McKinney.)

Former Royal Canadian Mounted Police officer and construction engineer James Mighten came to Chattanooga in the 1880s. The firm of McDaniel and Mighten built the Point Hotel. Incline No. 1 terminated inside the four-story, 58-room hotel. Termed "a palace set on a hill," by the *Chattanooga Times*, the hotel opened on May 28, 1888, and featured dining rooms, a billiard room, and a bathhouse. Nightly room rates ranged from $2.50 to $4. Theodore Roosevelt was a guest in 1902. (Courtesy of John Doyle.)

Measuring 4,360 feet in length, Incline No. 1 ascended a grade of 33 degrees over five trestles and two switchbacks. Two cable cars manufactured by the Wasson Car Company of Chattanooga carried 24 passengers in wooden, open-air cars with handrails for safety and side canvas curtains to keep out wind and rain. The railway also carried construction material up to the site of the Point Hotel.

Major King was the first passenger to ride Incline No. 1. Impatient for its completion and formal opening, he fastened two flatcars together and made the first round trip on December 9, 1886. The Incline officially opened on March 21, 1887. It closed in 1899.

In August 1885, construction began on an incline railroad from the present Thirty-eighth Street up Lookout Mountain. The Lookout Incline Railway Company completed what came to be called Incline No. 1 in March 1886. A round trip cost 50¢. In 1887, over 150,000 people made the scenic though somewhat frightening journey. This photograph shows the Incline No. 1 engine house at the foot of Lookout Mountain.

The Point Hotel opened in May 1888. Day visitors could purchase a round-trip ticket, ride the Incline, enter into the hotel at a 90-degree angle, have lunch at the hotel dining room, enjoy the spectacular views from the hotel's wraparound verandas, and return to the valley. A 15-minute schedule was maintained in order to accommodate the hotel visitors. In 1888, twenty-year-old J.B. Pound, eventual newspaper owner and hotel developer, decided to make his home in Chattanooga while admiring the scenery from the balcony.

Pres. Benjamin Harrison, in the front of the platform, visited Chattanooga in the fall of 1889. Two decorated electric streetcars, seen here parked in front of Incline No. 1, also held a number of local dignitaries, several of whom are identified: 1. Judge David Key; 2. Capt. Charles Lyerly; 3. Theodore Montague; 4. C.E. James; and 5. Charley Whiteside.

Even before the opening of Incline No. 1 and the Point Hotel, plans were being made to construct a narrow-gauge railway (track width less than 4.5 feet) from the Point Hotel across the top of Lookout Mountain to Sunset Rock. Pictured here is the terminal at Sunset Rock around 1886.

Referred to as the "Narrow Gauge," the tracks were eventually extended seven miles to the Natural Bridge, Lula Lake and the Lookout Inn. Skirting property owned by the Whitesides, the train ran along the west side of the ridge. An 11-ton engine pulled the railcars across several trestles, including Trestle No. 2, pictured here. This photograph shows the Narrow Gauge under construction.

By 1890, Incline No. 1 and the Narrow Gauge were opened. From the terminal in St. Elmo, visitors came up Lookout Mountain to the interior of the Point Hotel, and crossed the hotel station to connect with the Narrow Gauge. Despite efforts to keep them open, competition forced the closure of Incline No. 1 and the Point Hotel by 1900. The Narrow Gauge line continued to operate until the mid-1920s. The Point Hotel was razed in 1910.

Before the opening of Incline No. 1, plans were underway to build a broad-gauge railroad from St. Elmo to the top of Lookout Mountain. The Chattanooga and Lookout Mountain Railway investors included Chattanooga businessmen R.L. and Ed Watkins (pictured here) and C.E. James. Begun in June 1887 and completed in January 1889, the line passed along the base of Lookout Mountain to an area above the present Reflection Riding, where a switchback aimed the train up the remaining front of the mountain.

Completed in July 1889, the Broad Gauge Railroad (tracks wider than 4.5 feet) was owned by the Chattanooga & Lookout Mountain Railroad. Running from the Virginia Avenue and Fifth Street station, the line passed along the northern base of Lookout Mountain past the Cravens house, traveled over Incline No. 1, and doubled back in front of the Cravens house before making its way to the summit, ending just a few blocks from the present-day Point Park.

The right-of-way for the Broad Gauge and, later, the electric cars up Lookout Mountain cut through the property of the Cravens family. Pictured here, the Cravens home was destroyed during the Civil War and later by fire. Robert Cravens rebuilt the house, and his son, Jesse Cravens, negotiated permanent passes on the line for his family and descendants in exchange for the right of way across his property. Note the Iowa Civil War monument in the foreground and the New York monument in the background of this photograph.

With the opening of the Broad Gauge Railroad, tourists could come into Chattanooga's Union Station and, without transferring, proceed to the Mountain Junction Station (an early designation for the southern section of St. Elmo) at Virginia and Fifty-fifth Street and up Lookout Mountain to the Lookout Inn. Powered by the steam engine *Mississippi*, the Broad Gauge made daily trips hauling freight and passengers. In January 1889, on opening day, 6,000 people made the one-hour trip from downtown to the top of Lookout Mountain.

By summer 1889, the Chattanooga and Lookout Mountain Railroad Company began construction on the Lookout Inn, located across from the present Incline No. 2 terminal. A massive stone and wood structure, the 365-room hotel opened in 1890 and quickly became a popular resort, attracting visitors from over the world as well as the United States. Violinist Joseph Cadek came with the Boston Symphony Orchestra in 1893. He was so taken by the beauty of the area that he returned with his family and eventually opened the Cadek Music Conservatory.

The Lookout Inn played host to Presidents Grover Cleveland, William McKinley, and Theodore Roosevelt but was never financially profitable. By the time the hotel burned on November 17, 1908, in a spectacular fire seen all over the valley, the Broad Gauge had also ceased to operate. Using the Broad Gauge tracks, the Chattanooga Railway & Light Company operated an electric streetcar line from 1913 to 1920. Eventually, the tracks were torn up and sold for scrap.

Considered an engineering genius, Josephus Conn Guild Sr. helped design the Hale's Bar Dam and Incline No. 2, seen here under construction. The Guild Trail is named in honor of both J.C. Guild Sr. and his son J.C. Guild Jr., whose company eventually owned the Incline. The trail begins at Forty-seventh Street and Alabama Avenue and continues to the top of Lookout Mountain following the bed of the Broad Gauge Railroad.

In 1895, John Crass, Jesse Cravens, Linn White, Josephus Guild Sr., and members of the Whiteside family received a charter for the Lookout Incline & Lula Lake Railroad Company to build Incline No. 2. Completed in 90 days, by November 1895, the Incline operated from this site in St. Elmo, carrying passengers nine tenths of a mile with a 72-percent grade to the upper Lookout Mountain station 1,450 feet above St. Elmo. This 1910 postcard was sent to Hungary.

The Lookout Mountain Railroad Company designed Incline No. 2 to follow a straight line up Lookout Mountain, thus making the trip in the shortest amount of time over the shortest distance. The wooden cars were enclosed and powered by coal-fired steam engines. Small coal carriers were mounted on the front of each car to resupply the engines on each trip. The cars were converted to electric power in 1911. This 1909 postcard shows the observation deck on the rear of the car that provided a full view of the mountains and valley.

The original Incline No. 2 terminal was used from 1895 until 1949, when it was razed and a new terminal erected. Opened in time for the Incline's 54th anniversary, the dedication was attended by Jo Conn Guild Jr., son of the incline designer, and Mayor Hugh Wasson, descendant of the maker of the cars for Incline No. 1. Pictured here at the 1949 reopening of the Incline, Guild was president of the Chattanooga Railway & Light Company, later the Southern Coach Company, which owned the Incline for many years.

Although primarily a tourist attraction today, Incline No. 2 was, for many years, a primary source of transportation up and down Lookout Mountain. The Incline carried mail, workers to and from their jobs, high school and junior high school students, groceries from the A&P next door to the terminal, blocks of ice, and merchandise from the drugstores. This 1909 postcard shows the terminal at the top of Lookout Mountain.

Born within a block of the Incline terminal, Malcolm Bice began working for the railroad in 1933. He later recalled during the winter taking children's sleds up the Incline, where they began sliding down Lookout Mountain from Bragg Avenue, down Scenic Highway to its end in St. Elmo. Malcolm and his wife, Edith, lived only five blocks from the Incline on Alabama Avenue.

The Incline remains St. Elmo's most recognized feature. The rail line is considered to be the steepest and safest cable incline in the world. Now owned by Chattanooga Area Rapid Transit Authority, the Incline is actually a funicular: a cable railway on a steep incline with simultaneous ascending and descending cars balancing each other. The 1949 lower station was replaced in 1986 by the current station. The current cars were placed into service in 1987. The cables are replaced every two to three years.

Acquired by J.H. Warner in 1881, the Chattanooga Street Railroad consisted of several open wooden cars pulled by a horse or mule. Eventually extending from downtown Chattanooga to the foot of Lookout Mountain, the trip over mostly dirt roads was dusty and took nearly three hours. Although replacement of the horse or mule cars with electric cars began soon after 1881, horses and mules continued to pull the cars through city streets until 1891.

The Chattanooga Electric Railroad Line, with J.H. Warner as president, was established in 1878. Providing service throughout the city, the Lookout Mountain and St. Elmo Line began at the Market Street station, where the Chattanooga Choo-Choo is located today. The cars traveled 4.75 miles through Chattanooga and into St. Elmo, with stops at the Incline and Forest Hills Cemetery, terminating at the Virginia Avenue station. Opened in March 1886, the St. Elmo line was the first suburban line; thus St. Elmo became Chattanooga's first streetcar suburb.

Electric streetcars, called interurbans, continued to operate in and around Chattanooga, including St. Elmo, until 1947, when motorized buses took over the routes.

Founded in 1884, within three years the Union Railway Company, owned by C.E. James, was hauling freight around the city to the various factories and businesses using steam locomotives. Termed the "Belt Line," the railway soon began offering passenger service around the city. By 1889, the 29.9-mile line offered 128 daily round trips around Chattanooga, including trips to and from the Virginia Avenue depot in St. Elmo.

Ironically, C.E. James, one of Chattanooga's most successful entrepreneurs, reportedly believed that electric streetcars were a passing fad and did not modernize his rail line. By 1891, he had lost ownership of the Belt Line. Eventually, James became a believer in electric railways. In 1911, he organized the Chattanooga Traction Company to provide electric railroad service up Signal Mountain.

A.M. Johnson had Georgia Avenue (now St. Elmo Avenue) graded between First and Fifth Streets (now Forty-fifth Street) in order to begin construction on his new development. He also had a six-inch water main installed down Georgia Avenue by the City Water Company, of which he was president. Thus St. Elmo became the first suburb with city water. Street paving did not begin until St. Elmo was incorporated in 1905.

Tennessee and St. Elmo Avenues were paved by the mid-1920s, but side streets remained largely unpaved until the early 1940s. Unpaved dirt streets were often covered with a mixture of rocky dirt and gravel, giving them a white-yellow appearance. A steam shovel, sitting where St. Elmo Central is located today, loaded the material from a large pile into wagons or trucks that spread the mixture. The pile of material is shown here at the far right of this undated photograph. (Courtesy of Chattem Corporation.)

Seven

FOREST HILLS CEMETERY

Feeling that the growing city of Chattanooga needed a new municipal cemetery, 11 businessmen, including A.M. Johnson, met in 1874 to form a cemetery association. Each member of the association chipped in $3 to defray the cost of the charter. Adjacent to St. Elmo, the new cemetery eventually covered over 100 rolling acres. This photograph shows the cemetery around 1900. At this time, the cemetery had a small lake located close to the entrance gate, a gatehouse, a shelter house, and a home for the cemetery caretaker with a stable in the basement of the house.

Occupying approximately 100 acres, Forest Hills Cemetery has room for 70,000 graves, of which nearly 46,000 are occupied. When the cemetery opened, a number of families bought multiple plots, the largest of which has space for 85 graves. In 1890, single plots could be purchased for $5, and interment cost $2.50. In 1934, a single grave sold for $5, with an additional $14 to $19 for interment.

Initially, Forest Hills Cemetery had an on-site caretaker who lived with his family in this brick Victorian home located close to the cemetery entrance. The caretaker functioned as a cemetery superintendent, recording burials and sales of plots. The Fry family, pictured here in 1897, was among the first resident caretakers. Some of the bricks used in the construction of the current cemetery office are from this house, which was torn down in the 1940s. (Courtesy of the Community Association of Historic St. Elmo.)

Early cemetery caretakers were required to enter the cause of death in the cemetery ledger. Causes of death included yellow fever, old age (over 45), "crazy," gunshot wounds, hanging, and murder. Many babies and young children died of diseases like diphtheria, typhoid fever, scarlet fever, measles, and pneumonia. Women who died in childbirth and still-born births were also common.

During its early years of operation, the cemetery had a gatehouse at the entrance. Confederate veteran Gustavus Augustus "Henry" Gothard was one of the gatekeepers. Reared in Rhea County, by age 16, Henry was a scout for the Confederate army. As the cemetery gatekeeper, he rang the bell to signal the workers to retire as a funeral cortege approached and saluted the deceased as they passed. He also kept the skates and bicycles of the students at Lookout Junior High School safe in the guardhouse while they attended school.

Henry Clay Miller fought at the Battle of Chickamauga with the 81st Ohio Infantry. He liked the area, and when his son's health required a warmer climate, he and his wife, Rebecca, moved from Ohio to St. Elmo. They ran a general store on St. Elmo Avenue and lived for a while above the store. Eventually, the family moved to 4003 St. Elmo Avenue. Henry was the gatekeeper for the Forest Hills Cemetery from 1913 until his death in 1917. He is pictured here, wearing his gatekeeper's badge, with his wife, Rebecca. (Courtesy of Patricia Lewis.)

African Americans were buried in a segregated section of the cemetery from its opening until the 1960s. Early African American burials included George Nolan (1894), a railroad porter; Hiram Tyree (1926), a politician and longtime Chattanooga alderman; William Lewis (1896), a blacksmith; his nephew John Lovell (1898), owner of the Mahogany Ballroom on Cherry Street; and Randolph Miller (1916), owner of Chattanooga's first African American newspaper. The Lewis-Lovell family is pictured here about 1880.

The first person buried in the cemetery was Walter Hayter. Born in London, England, the 23-year-old engineer was hired by the cemetery association as a surveyor. When he died unexpectedly in his hotel room in 1880, the *Chattanooga Times* stated that "he had no one in the city to mourn him."

Purchased through a fund created by the police and fire departments, this section of the Forest Hills Cemetery was originally set aside for firemen and policemen killed in the line of duty. Currently, anyone who served in the fire and police departments can request burial in this section. The first men buried were Henry Iler and Matthew Peak, who died in the line of duty on June 9, 1887, during the Bee Hive Department Store fire.

Pictured here in 1934, Grace Moore, daughter of Loveman's Department Store owner Richard Moore, sang for 16 years with the Metropolitan Opera Company. Nominated for an Academy Award in 1935 for her performance in *One Night of Love*, she stared in a number of successful musical films. She was killed in a plane crash in 1947, and many people, including Jim Lee of St. Elmo, recall the crowds assembled to mourn her at the Chattanooga First Baptist Church and burial at Forest Hills Cemetery.

This 1930s side-opening hearse was used by Wann Funeral Home for a number of years. Once the casket was placed on the interior platform, it rotated into position within the hearse. (Courtesy of John Hargiss.)

Prior to the advent of the community-operated emergency medical system in the late 1960s, funeral homes provided ambulance services using largely untrained employees. This 1948 Cadillac hearse/ambulance was used by Wann Funeral Home. (Courtesy of John Hargiss.)

This monument was erected at the graves of Rob and Margaret Eldridge, who were killed in a car accident on December 26, 1948. Their youngest son, Jim, owns Ledco Construction Company, located on St. Elmo Avenue.

The Forest Hills Cemetery was at one time referred to as the "outdoor showroom" for the Coumolli Monument Company. Mario Coumolli's company, located on Broad Street, created many of the monuments in the cemetery. Reportedly, he was very proud of the one made for George Scholze.

Many symbols signifying information about the deceased or the feelings of the living are incorporated into grave markers. An anvil is a symbol for a blacksmith or the patron saint of blacksmiths, St. Eligus. The name of the deceased has worn away with time.

The angels with trumpets that adorn the monument erected by A.M. Johnson over the grave of his wife, Thankful, symbolize the departure of the soul from earth and its triumphant arrival into heaven.

The clasped hands, one feminine and one masculine, symbolizes matrimony, as with the wives of W.D. Davies. The graves of Maggie, who died in 1896, and Elen, who died in 1904, are marked with the same tombstone.

The eight points of the Maltese cross, chosen by the Tom Fritts family, represent the Beatitudes.

Alexander McPherson's monument has many symbols adorning the frequently used tree stone. The three links of a chain represent membership in the Independent Order of Odd Fellows, while the Latin cross represents Christianity. The fern symbolizes humility and sincerity, while the Easter lily represents purity and the casting off of earthly matters and attaining heavenly qualities.

The primary symbol of membership in the Freemasons is the square and compass with the letter "G," as seen on the Hartman family marker. The letter "G" may stand for God or geometry. The compass and square represent the interaction between mind and matter and refers to the progression from the material to the intellectual to the spiritual.

The symbol for the Woodmen of the World is used frequently on Forest Hills headstones. An insurance society, membership guaranteed that "no Woodman would rest in an unmarked grave." For a time the tree stone, a symbol for nature, was the marker of choice for members of the society, including H.C. May.

Marking the graves of the Joseph Cadek family, this stone features a possible depiction of one of the seven virtues, while the palm frond symbolizes the believer's triumph over death. The lyre is a symbol for the love of music.

The Latin cross mounted on three tiers, as seen on the marker of the Webster and Susie James family, is symbolic of the Trinity. This combination of the Latin cross with an angel mounted on three tiers also symbolizes the Cross of Calvary.

The caduceus is a symbol for the practice of medicine. This monument was erected at the grave of Dr. Melvin Binger by his "devoted patients."

This lovely monument seems to depict a likeness of Grace Oliver, who died at age 17. The lyre symbolizes a love of poetry and music.

Used frequently, the partially draped urn, as seen at the grave of Myra Peeples, symbolizes the lifting of the veil between earth and heaven.

St. Elmo resident Steve Sherfey placed a number of discarded cemetery monuments behind this home at 4501 Alabama Avenue as a joke on the Hall family, who lived there in the 1980s. Somehow, the yard was recorded by the state as a cemetery. People even claimed to have family members buried there. When the home was damaged during the April 2011 tornadoes, the current owner had great difficulty obtaining a building permit due to the recorded cemetery. The mistake was eventually corrected and the mystery of the "other" St. Elmo cemetery was solved.

Eight

THE FLOOD OF 1917

Prior to the construction of the Tennessee Valley Authority system of dams, the valley was subject to yearly spring flooding from heavy rains and snow melt. The March flood of 1917 was one of the worst on record and the highest the area had seen since 1886. The citizens of Chattanooga began to take notice when heavy rains caused the river to flood low-lying areas on March 4, 1917.

Flood stage on the Tennessee River at Chattanooga was 33 feet. By the morning of March 5, the river was over 39 feet. Two hundred families were forced to leave their homes. Most businesses were forced to close, including Bates Horse Shoeing at Market and Sixteenth Streets.

On March 5, the floodwaters were rising at the rate of two tenths of an inch per hour, with a crest of 45 feet predicted on March 7. The *Chattanooga Times*, the only method for quickly disseminating information, published information on which areas of the city would be affected and at what level. The St. Elmo area would be flooded at less than 45 feet. The *Chattanooga Times* continued to publish throughout the emergency.

The Milne Chair Company in East Chattanooga was surrounded by water on March 7. St. Elmo mayor and lumberyard owner Findley Seagle had wagons and boats quickly built in order to transport residents out of St. Elmo. (Courtesy of Helen Humphreys Johnson.)

Thirteen city schools and a number of churches were opened for those displaced by the flood, as city agencies mobilized for the impending disaster. City ambulances moved the sick from their homes. Several families afflicted with measles were taken to hospitals, as was a woman who had given birth as the water flooded her home.

Housed in Orange Grove Public School on Main Street with his three children, Tom Black, who called himself "a jack-leg preacher," told the *Chattanooga Times* on March 5 that he intended to "get busy and have a good meeting tonight. The folk is all here and can't get away and they'll jest have to listen. It ought to be a good chance to spread the gospel."

By the morning of March 6, at least 800 families, about 4,000 people, had been moved to safety. Many were housed in schools, churches, and vacant buildings that were taken over by the city. Orders from the police were required to get some people to move. The *Chattanooga Times* reported that women wept as their homes were flooded.

Fifty percent of the city and the area south of Main Street to the Georgia line were inundated as the river rose to over 43 feet on March 6. The view from Cameron Hill showed a submerged Chattanooga Island (McClellan Island) as the swirling dirty yellow water covered the toe of Moccasin Bend. Water climbed the approach to the new Market Street Bridge. City commissioner E.R. Betterton called for every truck and wagon to be available to assist those fleeing from the flood.

As floodwaters continued to rise by early March 6, Southern Saddlery was underwater, and the bridge over Whiteside Street (Broad Street) was within 18 inches of being overtopped, thus closing travel by vehicle into the city. Mayor Seagle arranged for the Southern Railroad to stop close to St. Elmo in order evacuate the community.

On March 6, the St. Elmo Colored School on Thirty-eighth Street housed the black residents of St. Elmo while the North St. Elmo School (middle of photograph) housed the white residents. Residents brought as much as they could with them, including pets and chickens. Mayor Finley reported that "Many of those marooned seemed stupefied by the prospect before them, and that strenuous effort was required to rescue them."

Streetcar and auto access to St. Elmo was impossible by March 6. Mayor Seagle, in cooperation with Newell Sanders of the Nashville, Chattanooga & St. Louis Railroad, instituted the St. Elmo Special, offering free emergency service to and from St. Elmo every hour from Union Station, stopping at all of the cross streets not under water. The *Chattanooga Times* reported, "Hundreds of people took advantage of the service. . . . No sightseeing parties were allowed."

On the evening of March 6, fifty percent of the city was flooded, including the area below Main Street to the Georgia line. Endurance Field (Engle Stadium) was completely submerged. John Stagmaier, chairman of the Food Relief of Chattanooga, reported that "over three thousand meals were supplied by various churches around the city."

Early morning on March 7, the river crested at 47.7 feet. Six thousand people were homeless. Ferger Place was the only dry spot south of Main Street. Filled with refugees, the first and second floors of the Orange Grove Public School on Main Street were flooded. All evacuees were moved to the third floor. The armory on Market Street sheltered many black families. Warner Park, the low point on McCallie Avenue, was under water.

With all of the schools (save one) flooded or in use as a refuge, students and teachers joined the relief efforts. Girls helped to prepare food, while the boys helped make wooden flatboats. Some of the boys joined with the Humane Society to rescue pets and other animals. In St. Elmo, Boy Scouts under the leadership of C.C. Varnell and Rudd Lordor rescued six pigs from a water-filled house using a skiff.

Water broke through into the Citico railroad yard as freight cars were shunted to higher ground. A railroad watchman had to be rescued when the watchtower was completely surrounded. The area around Orchard Knob was a sea of muddy water, as was Rossville, Clifton Hills, Alton Park, and St. Elmo. Alice Humphreys observed on March 7 that the water over the bridge at Burnt Mill Creek rose in only two days. (Courtesy of Helen Humphreys Johnson.)

On March 8, after a brief stationary period, the river began to fall. A general health committee headed by G.W. Knight was appointed to conduct an extensive clean-up of every block of the city and suburbs. It took three days for the river to return to its banks. As the water began to recede, 575 people were housed in the courthouse.

A steady fall of rain on March 8 added to the misery and slowed the river's fall. The relief committee called for more volunteer workers, as those who had been working since the river overtopped its banks were "much fatigued." Throughout the emergency, the supply of food and coal was normal, as merchants worked diligently to distribute supplies wherever needed.

Seventy-three of the men who volunteered during the flood formed an organization they named STI, or Stick-to-It's. After the crisis passed, they held a final meeting "to surrender police badges, rubber boots, and slickers." A number of these men lived in the St. Elmo community.

A relief committee was formed under the leadership of J.F. Finlay and Z.C. Patten Jr. in order to raise money for flood relief. Chattanoogans were characteristically generous, and over $20,500 was raised. The estimated total flood damage was nearly $300,000. There was only one fatality.

BIBLIOGRAPHY

Allen, Penelope Johnson. *Genealogy of a Branch of the Johnson Family and Connections.* Revised and continued by Helen Miller Betts. Chattanooga: n.p., 1967.

Armstrong, Zella. *The History of Hamilton County and Chattanooga, Tennessee, Volumes I and II.* Lookout Mountain, TN: Lookout Mountain Publishing, 1931.

Byrum, C. Stephen. *A History of the Chattanooga District of the United Methodist Church.* Chattanooga: Paida Productions, 1988.

Chattanooga Free Press

Chattanooga Times

Chattanoogan.com

Douthat, James, Judy Harris, and Frankie Pope. *The St. Elmo Story.* Chattanooga: St. Elmo Improvement League, 1986.

Desmond, Jerry. *Chattanooga.* Charleston, SC: Arcadia Publishing, 1996.

Gammon, Wirt. *Your Lookouts Since 1885.* Chattanooga, TN: n.p., 1952.

Gaston, Kay Baker. "The Remarkable Harriet Whiteside." *Tennessee Historical Quarterly,* Winter 1981.

Hughes, Nathaniel C. Jr., and John Wilson. *The Confederate Soldiers of Hamilton County, Tennessee.* Signal Mountain, TN: Mountain Press, 2001.

Jenkins, Gary. *The Johnson House of St. Elmo.* Chattanooga: n.p., 2009.

Keister, Douglas. *Stories in Stone.* Salt Lake City: Gibbs Smith Publisher, 2009.

Livingood, James. *A History of Hamilton County, Tennessee.* Memphis: Memphis State University Press, 1981.

Walker, Alan A. *Railroads of Chattanooga.* Charleston, SC: Arcadia Publishing, 2003

Ware, Jennifer, Arline Caldwell, and Sarah DeWaters. *The St. Elmo Story.* (2nd ed.) Chattanooga: The Community Association of Historic St. Elmo, 2007.

White, J. Bliss. *1904 Biography and Achievements of the Colored Citizens of Chattanooga.* Signal Mountain, TN: Mountain Press, 2004 (reprinted).

Wilson, John. *Chattanooga's Story.* Chattanooga: Roy McDonald Publisher, 1980.

———. *Lookout.* Chattanooga: Roy McDonald Publisher, 1977.

———. *The Patten Chronicle.* Chattanooga: Roy McDonald Publisher, n.d.

Visit us at
arcadiapublishing.com
....

Printed in the USA
CPSIA information can be obtained
at www.ICGtesting.com
LVHW070354180124
769031LV00008B/204